ROBUSTO MAKING FRIENDS

By Zhi Liu Martin

Assistance From Fiona Cook

刘智出品

Vermont, U.S.A

Robusto, an alpaca, used to live at Grandma Jennifer's farm in Vermont. It has beautiful scenery and a large grass field. Robusto's life was very happy because he was living with his family.

One day, Grandma Jennifer sent Robusto to Uncle Tom 's ranch. Uncle Tom's ranch raised many chickens and ducks, but the dog, Shadow, was getting very old and couldn't protect the small animals like before. Robusto, the alpaca, got a job as a guardian.

Robusto takes care of and protects small animals. The chickens like having Robusto around.

Small animals feel very safe with Robusto near. Young turkeys often lean on Robusto's side and fall asleep. Robusto wants the young turkey to sleep well, so he keeps his legs motionless, and keeps turning his head, surveying the surroundings.

But when there are two tall horses off to Robusto's side, he always turned to look at them. They are so proud and powerful. Robusto envies them and likes them.

Gradually, Robusto pays more and more attention to the two horses. He wants to be friends with them, but the horses are very arrogant. How can the horses accept Robusto?

Robusto is a clever boy, so soon he has a plan.

One day, the horses were eating the grass quietly in the south field as usual.

Suddenly the horses found the alpaca had secretly come up behind them. He was also focusing on eating the grass.

The horses were scared, and quickly ran away. Horses are not arrogant , but very timid and afraid of strange animals. Robusto's plan had failed.

Robusto was alone and unhappy walking on the road, Uncle Tom drove a tractor past him, and asked,

"Robusto, why are you unhappy?"

"Because the horses would not make friends with me."

"The horses use their sense of smell to recognize friends. Do you have a friendly smell?"

Robusto lay on the ground thinking about Uncle Tom's words. He did not understand what the friendly smell is.

An old hen passed by.

She said, "a friendly smell is one that is familiar to the horses. It is full of love and sharing, and shows no harm."

Robusto followed the horses, but not too closely. The horses were not frightened. They stood there, sniffing the air with the smell of Robusto. There was no danger. It was a safe smell.

In the evening, Robusto usually slept in front of Uncle Tom's house. Now he slept in the hay barn, his smell would be on the hay that horses eat.

A few days later, the horses ate the hay and accepted the smell of Robusto.

Robusto tried to stand near the horses. The horses were not scared, and they continued eating.

One day, the horses allowed Robusto to eat grass with them, although they still maintained a distance.

Robusto was very happy. His plan was working.

The horses were more comfortable to have Robusto near, but they were still not friends.

Robusto didn't have a sharing smell. He decided to share his favorite food, a box of apples, with the horses.

"Lena, Mandy, would you like to eat the apples with me?" said Robusto.

Mandy smelled the box. It was filled with apples. Mandy was very happy, that is the horse's favorite food also. Then they ate apples together.

One day when Robusto was resting, Mandy came up close behind him, and smelled him. It was a familiar smell, a sharing smell, and a friendly smell.

From that moment on, Robusto was good friends with the horses, and they have a close relationship.

Every day they play and laugh together. Sometimes Robusto rolls on the ground, and Mandy looks at him and smiles. Their days together are fun.

One day, the horses and Robusto were eating grass, when suddenly they smelled some other horses on the farm. They looked nervously in that direction.

Two new horses came to the ranch. They are polo ponies. Supressa has a mysterious black mane, and Olga is taller with a white star on her forehead. It was a new place for them, they were nervous and excited. They smelled other animals.

Mandy quickly ran over, and Robusto followed behind to meet the new horses.

Mandy approached Olga, and smelled her.
Yes, the horse smell, a friend's smell.

Mandy came close to Supressa and sniffed. She realized Supressa would be her boss. This is the horse's nature.

The two new horses smelled Mandy in return, and felt safe. But they did not know Robusto. They looked at him nervously.

Robusto drew close to Olga and said,
    "Hi, friend, I am an alpaca, I will be your friend.
You can smell me."
    Olga cautiously sniffed Robusto. It is a new smell,
an alpaca smell.

Robusto walked over to Supressa, "Hi, friend. I am a smart alpaca. I can protect you. Do you want to make friends with me? You can smell me."

Supressa came close to Robusto and smelled him. Only alpaca scent!

"Robusto is our friend, he can see far away. If there is a dangerous animal coming, he will sound the alarm." Mandy said to the new horses. Supressa smiled and nodded.

The two new horses were no longer afraid, but they were still very nervous, because they don't know what an alpaca is. They kept watching Robusto. But one day things changed.

On that day, Uncle Tom and his friends went for a short trek on the horses. It would be a difficult trip for the horses, because the trails were muddy and rocky.

They rode the horses along the rugged mountain road. Robusto followed behind.

The horses were struggling to walk through the mud because the trail was slippery. Robusto still followed, even though the trail was difficult for him too.

Supressa asked Robusto why he followed them. Robusto replied, "I want to be with my friends." Supressa approached Robusto again, and smelled him. She sensed a caring smell, a friendship smell.

Olga also sniffed Robusto again. Now she recognized the smell of friendship.

In the sunshine, Robusto lay on the ground and watched his horse friends. He enjoyed this moment very much.

Since then, the four and a half horses have happily lived together. Robusto is, of course, the half horse!

Photography records every moment, tells the true story, shows good things.

ISBN : 978-1546436393

Printed in the U.S.A.

刘智出品
Vermont, U.S.A